WHAT WOULD
CHARLIE SHEEN
DO?

'I'M NOT THOMAS JEFFERSON.
HE WAS A PUSSY.'

Carlos Irwin Estevez, aka **Charlie Sheen**, *2011*

What Would Charlie Sheen Do?

Published in the UK in 2012 by
Punk Publishing Ltd, 3 The Yard, Pegasus Place, London SE11 5SD

www.punkpublishing.co.uk
www.wwcsdo.com

Copyright © Punk Publishing Ltd 2012

A catalogue record of this book is available from the British Library.

ISBN 978-1-906889-55-5
10 9 8 7 6 5 4 3 2 1

WHAT WOULD CHARLIE SHEEN DO?

WINNING WORDS OF WISDOM

S R Dawson

With illustrations by
Jake Ayres

'MY BRAIN FIRES IN A WAY
THAT MAYBE ISN'T FROM THIS
TERRESTRIAL REALM.'

CONTENTS

'I WANT TO DELIVER SOME **SHIT**, AND I WANT TO DELIVER IT IN THE WAY THAT IS FREAKIN... IN THE EPICENTER OF HOW I DELIVER THINGS, WHICH IS PERFECT AND TRUTHFUL AND RADICAL AND IN YOUR FACE. SO FAR IN YOUR FACE IT GRABS YOUR TEETH AND SHOVES THEM DOWN YOUR **FREAKIN THROAT** AND YOU'RE LIKE 'OH, WHAT A LOVELY LITTLE SNACK — IT TASTES LIKE MY TEETH BUT I DON'T CARE, BECAUSE **SHEEN** DELIVERED IT.''

WORK

'I WILL NOT WASTE MY PRECIOUS TIME.'

I overslept and am running late for a meeting. My (male) boss rings.

TELL HIM YOU'VE BEEN TURNING HIS TIN
CANS INTO **PURE GOLD** FOR THE PAST 8
YEARS (EVEN IF THIS DATE ISN'T RIGHT, GO
WITH IT ANYWAY — IT'LL CONFUSE HIS UNEVOLVED
MIND) AND IF HE'S GOT ANY SENSE HE'LL QUIT
BOTHERING YOU WHILE YOU TRY TO GET
THERE AND SAVE HIS ASS SOME MORE.

WINNING.

I overslept and am running late for a meeting. My (female) boss rings.

TELL HER YOU DIDN'T SLEEP A WINK BECAUSE YOU COULDN'T STOP THINKING ABOUT HER AND YOU WERE WORRIED IT WAS LOVE. SO YOU JUST SPENT THE PAST HOUR LOCKED IN YOUR HOME TRYING TO OVERCOME IT. BUT HERE'S THE GOOD NEWS:

THIS ROCKSTAR HAS CURED HIMSELF.

WINNING.

I partied super-hard last weekend and have just been told that all employees will undergo a compulsory drugs test in the next couple of days.

SOMEBODY BRING ME A FREAKIN CHALLENGE. So you overdid it a little, but I gotta ask: WERE YOU BANGING 7-GRAM ROCKS AND FINISHING THEM?

NO? Didn't think so.

If you can't get away with swapping urine samples with the nerdy office pussy then just grow some **COJONES** and say this: I am on a drug — IT'S CALLED **WINNING** — and you can't have any.

I've got a huge presentation to do in front of our most important clients next week and I'm TERRIFIED.

COME ON BRO. I WON 'BEST PICTURE' AT 20 — WASN'T EVEN TRYING — SO YOU CAN GET IT TOGETHER LONG ENOUGH TO SPIN SOME GNARLY WORDS AT A FEW MEASLY LOSERS. JUST REMEMBER THAT THEY WILL TUNE OUT AT SOME POINT BECAUSE THEY'RE **STUPID**, SO STICK IN SOME SNAPPY SHIT EVERY NOW AND AGAIN.

OH, AND STAY AWAY FROM THE CRACK BEFOREHAND, UNLESS YOU CAN MANAGE IT SOCIALLY. IF YOU CAN MANAGE IT SOCIALLY THEN GO FOR IT; IT'LL CALM YOUR NERVES. BUT NOT A LOT OF PEOPLE CAN, YOU KNOW.

I'm falling behind badly with work, but I'm too afraid to tell the boss in case I get fired.

You, sir, are a COWARD in a cheap suit. And now your gutlessness has blown up in your face — **LIKE AN EXPLODING CRACK PIPE.** I'm not gonna help you, I'm gonna hang out with these two smoking hotties and fly privately around the world. JEALOUS?

I used to love my job, but these days I'm so bored with it. We're in a recession, though, so I'm not sure whether to stay or boldly go...

GO. DON'T JUST SETTLE LIKE SOME DUMBASS SHEEP. OR NEXT THING, YOU'LL SUDDENLY WAKE UP TO FIND YOU'VE BEEN ASLEEP FOR 40 YEARS. QUIT IMMEDIATELY AND GO FIND YOURSELF SOME BADASS JOB. DO IT WITH ZEAL, WITH FOCUS, AND WITH... VIOLENT HATRED OF THIS SICK AND EXPLOITATIVE SYSTEM WE CALL 9 TO 5.

I'm a teacher and struggle to control the kids in my class. It's like they're out to make me cry.

PUH-LEEEEASE! Of COURSE THEY'RE OUT TO MAKE YOU CRY. RUGRATS ARE DEVIOUS LIKE THAT. MY ADVICE? BEAT THEM AT THEIR OWN GAME. GO **PLATOON** ON THEIR ASSES IF THEY EVEN LOOK LIKE THEY WANT TO STEP OUT OF LINE. LAY THE SMACKDOWN AND THEY WILL LEARN TO RESPECT THEIR GNARLY KICKASS TEACHER.

I got a low score in my latest evaluation.

TELL YOUR BOSS TO FUCK OFF. IT's **OVER**.
HE's WASTING YOUR PRECIOUS TIME.
YOU'RE A GNARLY GNARLINGTON. A
VATICAN ASSASSIN WARLOCK WITH MAGIC
AND POETRY AT YOUR FINGERTIPS.

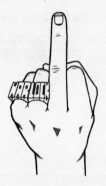

IF THAT DOESN'T MAKE HIM SIT BACK
AND SEE YOU FOR THE MAN YOU ARE,
THEN DEMAND A 50% PAY RISE. **STAT**.
HE'LL SEE WHO THE **WINNER** IS.

I told my boss to FUCK OFF, and lost my job.

PEOPLE TAKE EVERYTHING SO LITERALLY.
SHUT UP AND MOVE FORWARD.
OR FILE A WRONGFUL TERMINATION LAWSUIT.

I've been unemployed for over a year now. At the beginning, I was very proactive with searching and applying for jobs, but for the past four months I've lost all motivation and can't be bothered.

It's just that kind of defeatist attitude THAT MAKES ME **SICK**. Everything around you **SUCKS** and you just accept it and don't move forward and think that's how it's supposed to be? I DON'T BUY IT, I don't agree with it, I don't trust it, I don't care about it. **WINNERS** don't just give up, buddy. Now **MAN UP** and PUT YOURSELF OUT THERE, or I'll be sending one of my secret assassins to give you the wake-up call you OBVIOUSLY need.

I dread meetings with my boss because all he does is stare at my breasts – even when he's talking to me. I've taken to wearing turtlenecks but this has done nothing to discourage him. He's also far too touchy-feely for my liking.

TASER.

MONEY

'I'M GIVING TO THEM I GUESS WHAT THEY WANT BUT NOT NECESSARILY WHAT THEY CAN HANDLE — **PUSSIES!**'

I'm a shopaholic. And I don't mean that in an endearing, Isla Fisher-type sense – I mean I have a serious problem. My credit cards are all maxed out and I'm in serious trouble.

I don't count my days because it puts such a PREMIUM on them and you run around with your days going 'WHOA don't lose your days, DON'T LOSE YOUR DAYS. BOOM — I've lost my days.' And then it's like, 'Where'd my days go?' The same principle applies to money and spending.

I'm fed up with not earning any money. Even if I move jobs the pay doesn't get much better. The industry I'm in is just a notoriously badly paid one – so I'm told.

THIS IS A **NO-BRAINER**. RETRAIN AS AN ASSASSIN: JOB SATISFACTION AND FINANCIAL REWARDS IN ONE KICKASS, GNARLY JOB. IF YOU WANT RELIGION THROWN IN, THEN APPLY TO THE VATICAN.

A friend of mine wants to borrow a substantial amount of money from me. I want to help out, but am concerned he's not going to be able to pay me back when the time comes.

Ask yourself this: is my FRIEND more important, or my MONEY? If your answer's money, you shouldn't be reading this — you're a **DOUCHEBAG**. If it's your friend, then give him the money, but with a warning attached: PAY ME BACK or WATCH ME BURY YOU. Simple.

I've recently inherited a lump sum – which is great, but I'm not sure how to use it wisely: invest in property, or shares, or art, or even gold…

CHARLIE SHEEN MOVIES.

CHARLIE SHEEN MERCHANDISE.

AN F18.

LOVE

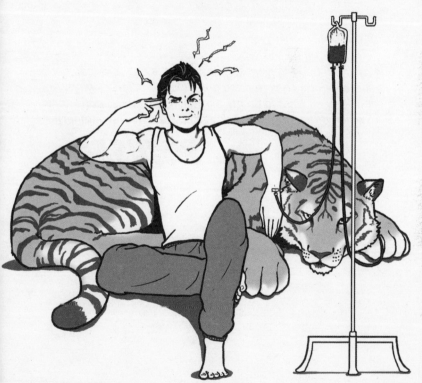

51

I joined a dating website a few months ago and met four different girls. They're each great in their different ways, but now they all want to be my exclusive girlfriend. I don't know which one to pick (they don't know about one another)!

WWCSD?

SLICED BREAD, MY MAN! YOU'RE NOT EVEN **BI-WINNING**, YOU'RE FREAKIN **QUAD-WINNING!** ONLY A **LOSER** WOULD SEE THIS AS A PROBLEM.

I really like this guy from work. We flirt at the coffee machine every day, and I think he's into me, but this has been going on for ages and he hasn't made a move yet.

THE GUY SOUNDS LIKE A PRIZE **PUSSY** TO ME. IF HE HASN'T POUNCED LIKE A HOT-BLOODED TIGER YET, YOU NEED TO STOP WASTING YOUR TIME ON HIM. **STOP DRINKING COFFEE.** MOVE ON.

My girlfriend dumped me. I feel so alone right now.

GROW SOME **BALLS**, BRO.
DEFEAT IS NOT AN
OPTION. I DEAL WITH FOOLS
AND TROLLS ALL THE
TIME, BUT YOU KNOW
WHAT? **WINNING**!
TURN THAT WEASEL
BLOOD INTO TIGER
BLOOD AND GO
GET YOURSELF A NEW
GODDESS. HELL, GO OUT
THERE AND GET YOURSELF
TWO NEW GODDESSES.

*I just saw my ex on the bus with his new girlfriend.
I was looking awful (no make-up) whereas she looked
pristine, and he gave me a look of triumph. I feel sick.*

You know what? You gotta MOVE ON, and I mean **NOW**. So you saw him and his SLUTFACED NEW HO — so freakin WHAT? Time to channel that inner goddess and exude some self-esteem before the trolls get you. 'Intimidation' is just another word for 'weak' and 'panic' is another word for 'pussy.' **ARE YOU A WEAK PUSSY?** Absofuckinlutely NOT, sister. Ride that bus with pride and you'll have **WON**. They will LOSE the rest of their lives as they think about YOU.

I'm always too nervous to go talk to girls when I'm out.

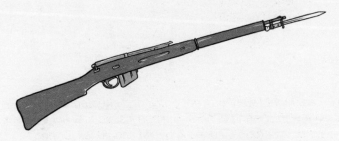

BE A FREAKIN **BAYONET**.

Last night I went out, got drunk and cheated on my wife with a friend of hers. But she kissed me, not the other way round. I don't know if I should tell, or not.

'I CAN'T BE BLAMED FOR MY IGNORANCE.' OH YEAH, WELL WHO ELSE AM I GONNA BLAME? **YOUR STUPID WIFE?** WHAT YOU'RE SAYING IS ROOTED IN VINTAGE BALDERDASH. YOU CHEATED ON YOUR WIFE. **DEAL WITH IT.** DON'T COME TO **CHARLIE SHEEN** FOR REDEMPTION — THAT'S THE BASKET THEY PUT ALL THE EGGS IN. (THAT'S A WEIRD METAPHOR, BY THE WAY. WOW.)

I've been in love with my best friend since we first met. It's been so long now that I don't know how to broach the subject without ruining our friendship (btw, I'm a girl and he's a guy).

LEMME TELL YOU SOMETHING, SISTER. WHOEVER SAID 'IGNORANCE IS BLISS' WAS OUT OF THEIR FREAKIN TREE. IT'S A MANTRA WORSHIPPED BY **STUPID PEOPLE**. AND IT IS THEIR FAULT, GODDAMNIT, FOR SITUATIONS SUCH AS THESE. IF YOU'RE NOT ALREADY RUNNING OFF TO TELL HIM YOU WANNA JUMP HIM RIGHT NOW, THEN I URGE YOU TO MAKE PLANS AND DO THIS **TONIGHT**.

*I think my boyfriend's cheating on me but
I don't have any solid evidence.*

IF YOU HAD PROOF, YOU KNOW THE ANSWER
WOULD BE: **TASER**; INSTEAD, IT'S TIME TO
START SHAKIN A TREE — AND BY THAT
I MEAN SHAKIN ALL THE TREES. REMEMBER,
A GUNSHOT IN THE MORNING WILL WAKE HIM
UP BETTER THAN A NICE CUP OF COFFEE.

SEX

'LET'S JUST HOOK UP AND
BRING FIERY DEATH.'

My girlfriend complains that when we're 'making love' I look furious and it puts her off.

COMMON PROBLEM, BRO. PASSION IS ALWAYS BEING MISINTERPRETED AS ANGER (LOOK AT ME). IF SHE CAN'T HANDLE YOUR **ROCKSTAR PASSION** IN

THOSE INTIMATE MOMENTS THEN SHE'S JUST GONNA HAVE TO SHUT HER EYES OR COVER HER FACE WITH SOMETHING — PREFERABLY A PICTURE OF SOMEONE WAY HOTTER. You'VE GOT ADONIS DNA, MY FRIEND, AND SHE CAN'T HANDLE IT.

My girlfriend isn't interested in sex anymore. Whenever
I make a move she just pushes me away – even
if I've done something really romantic like let her
have charge of the TV remote all evening.

You need to dump some ROCKET FUEL on this situation. AND **FAST**. Frankly, dude, this is a tough one because this sort of thing NEVER happens to me — I got girls lining up around the block for just a PIT-SNIFF of this rockstar's body. **I'M AN F18**, man — try it, if you dare. Go out with a porn star instead; you know what you're getting before you meet 'em. They're the best at what they do and I'm the best at what I do. And together it's, like... it's ON. (Sorry Middle America, YEAH I SAID IT.)

*My boyfriend wants me to have a breast enlargement.
He's even said he'll pay for it. I don't want the
surgery but am worried he'll leave me if I say no.*

EASY. SAY YES — ON ONE
CONDITION: HE GETS A
PENIS ENLARGEMENT AT THE
SAME TIME. **WINNING**.

I've recently started seeing a guy who's 20 years older than me. I really like him but have my reservations about sleeping with someone who's got wrinkles…

WWCSD?

Lemme put it in these terms for your **UNEVOLVED** mind: Grape juice or vintage wine? Cheap plastic SHIT or handcrafted antique furniture? Protection from a rookie cop or a gnarly WARLOCK, like Steven Seagal, Sly Stallone or **CHARLIE SHEEN**? There's a reason why the word EXPERIENCE got created, sweetheart. It puts the 'ex' into 'GREAT SEX.'

My girlfriend is really into role-play, which is cool, but I'm running out of inspiration. Doctor–Nurse: done; Teacher–Schoolgirl: done; Dolphin–Rainbow: done. I could go on…

THIS IS LIKE A SOBER ACID TRIP, BRO! I'D LIKE TO MEET YOUR GIRLFRIEND SOMEDAY... HERE'S ONE **GUARANTEED** TO KEEP HER OCCUPIED FOR SOME DAYS, IF YOU KNOW WHAT I MEAN... **CHARLIE SHEEN-GODDESS** (ANOTHER IF YOU CAN FIND A FRIEND.) YOU'RE GONNA **WIN** LIKE THERE'S NO TOMORROW. **SERIOUSLY.**

81

HEALTH

'THE ONLY THING I'M ADDICTED
TO RIGHT NOW IS **WINNING.**'

I'm worried I might be bi-polar.

WWCSD?

BI-POLAR – **BI-SCHMOLAR**. THE ONLY
THING YOU'RE DOING IS **BI-WINNING**.

I'm overweight and, no matter how many diets I try, I can't seem to slim down.

WWCSD?

Listen, buddy: 'Can't' is the **CANCER** of 'Happen.' The Nike slogan doesn't go 'Just **TRY** it.' Quit moaning about it and **DO** it. Make that fat ass SWEAT. (I work out TWICE a day but only one of those times is in the gym — d'you know what I'm saying? Having **TWO** goddesses in your life would help IMMEASURABLY with your weight-loss.)

I've struggled in the past with low self-esteem, but have been making good ground in overcoming my confidence issues. Sometimes I worry about overstepping the mark between confidence and arrogance, though.

You are who you are, bro. I've got a 10,000-year-old brain and the boogers of a 7 year-old. That's how I describe myself. And, I dunno man, I guess I'm just so GODDAMN BITCHIN AND INTERESTING that I exude confidence, but not in a way that makes people feel uncomfortable with my superiority.

I suffer from terrible insomnia. I've tried everything, but still sleep evades me.

Quit whining. You have a gift, a **WINNER'S** ADVANTAGE over most people. You know what? I don't sleep either. I WAIT. I wait, I think, and I DO AWESOME. GNARLY. SHIT. During sleep, you're inactive; you're losing time. So why waste this opportunity of wakefulness on worrying about it? You need to see that cup as being more than HALF **FREAKIN** FULL, BRO.

I'm ill all the time! Whatever bug might be doing the rounds, I always get it. This year I've felt like I've been permanently sick. I don't understand – I work out regularly, eat well and get enough sleep.

SOUNDS TO ME LIKE THE ONLY SICKNESS YOU'VE GOT IS YOUR MIND, BUDDY. SELF-PITY IS A RETARDED MANTRA. WHAT YOU NEED ISN'T MEDICINE; IT'S A DOSE OF **CHARLIE SHEEN**, SO LISTEN UP: **BOOM**! YOU'RE CURED.

HOME

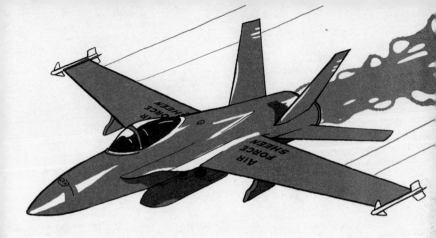

'I'M AN **F18**, MAN.
WATCH ME BURY YOU.'

My girlfriend has demanded no more Guys' Nights since the last poker night ended with Ralph vomiting on her favorite Teddy Bear and Hugo pissing in her wardrobe.

BULL S.H.I.T. WHEN YOU PEOPLE-PLEASE YOUR SOUL IS **DEAD**. YOU'VE GOT TO TAKE CARE OF YOURSELF. TELL HER TO SHUT HER TRAP, PUT DOWN HER MCDONALD'S, HER VACCINES AND HER COPY OF *THE NATIONAL ENQUIRER* AND FOCUS ON SOMETHING THAT MATTERS. SHE HAS THE RIGHT TO **KILL** YOU, BUT NOT THE RIGHT TO **JUDGE** YOU (OR YOUR BROS).

My roommates are so inconsiderate. I'm the only one who cleans the house (despite constantly asking them to help out) and I'm fed up. Should I suggest a roster?

ENOUGH ALREADY WITH THE
WEASELY WHINING. THIS
SMACKS OF **PUSSINESS**. GET
THE BLEACH OUT AND GO ON A
RAMPAGE AROUND THE HOUSE WITH IT
LIKE YOU'RE WIELDING NAPALM.
THEN WRITE THEM A MESSAGE IN BLOOD
(OR BLEACH, LIPSTICK OR, HEY, URINE) TO
THE LINES OF: **CLEAN UP OR DIE**. DUSTED.

103

My wife thinks I spend every Saturday morning cleaning our house while she's at the gym. In reality, I hired a cleaner and go sit in Starbucks. Thing is, we can't really afford it and I'm worried my wife will find out and go ape.

That, my gnarly friend, is an EXPERT MOVE by a seasoned professional. You lead by example. It's all about living on the edge, pushing the boundaries — even in some dull old domestic situation. Take me, for example: I don't live in the middle anymore because that's where you get SLAUGHTERED, that's when you get embarrassed in front of the prom queen. It's **NOT** an option.

If your wife does find out and unleashes hell, tell her to WIND IT IN and be happy that you're thoughtful and caring enough to get the house cleaned. HOW IT HAPPENED is **IRRELEVANT**.

My roommate eats my food (without asking) and uses my toiletries (again, without asking). I've already questioned him about it, but he just denies it. But there's no one else in the house, and it's driving me mad!

TASER.

FAMILY

'THOUGHT YOU WERE JUST
MESSING WITH ONE DUDE?'

My mom and I constantly bicker, and I'm fed up with it.

YOU HAVE TO HATE EVERYBODY THAT'S NOT IN YOUR FAMILY BECAUSE THEY'RE THERE TO DESTROY YOUR FAMILY. SO IT'S SIMPLE: **BE NICER TO YOUR MOM.**

My sister keeps borrowing my clothes without asking, and it's driving me nuts.

WWCSD?

PUT A HIT OUT ON HER. **STAT.** I'LL GET MY GNARLY CADRE OF ASSASSINS ON THE CASE.

*I'm desperate to come out of the closet, but
I'm petrified of my family's reaction.*

FIRSTLY, OBVIOUSLY, IT'S INSANE TO THINK I'D
HAVE THIS KIND OF PROBLEM: A) I'M A ROCKSTAR
LOVER WITH GODDESSES CONSTANTLY KNEELING
BEFORE ME, AND, B) I'M SCARED OF NO-ONE:
I'M **CHARLIE SHEEN**. SECONDLY, QUIT HIDING
— IT'S EMBARRASSING DUDE. NEXT SUBJECT.

*I've got two teenage boys with whom I seem
to have nothing in common. I'm always making
an effort with them but get nothing back.*

Dude. In order to demand their respect you need your kids to think of you in these kinds of **WINNING** terms: 'we need his wisdom and his bitchinness.' Respect doesn't grow on trees. You earn it through **GNARLY** endeavors — by being the kind of rockstar-assassin children look up to. Have them throw a BITCHIN party at your house and **JOIN IN**. Make sure you cut it just right — A SHAMEFUL TRAINWRECK FILLED WITH BLIND CUDDLY PUPPIES — that kind of affair. Next morning, you'll be THE DADDY. Trust me.

My husband and I are constantly fighting. Last week it was about what kind of lighting to go for; this week it's whether to go for marble or granite surfaces. (We're having our kitchen re-done.) I can't bear it any more.

LADY, THAT WOULD IMPLY
THAT I CARE ABOUT ORANGE
JUICE AND I HAVE A KITCHEN.
NEXT QUESTION.

FRIENDS

'EVERY GREAT MOVEMENT BEGINS WITH ONE MAN, AND I GUESS THAT'S ME.'

I earn a lot more money than my friends, and it's causing issues. I never show off about it – in fact I play it down – but they make snide comments all the time, and it's starting to really upset me.

JUST BECAUSE THEY LOOK LIKE DROOPY-EYED, ARMLESS CHILDREN NEXT TO YOU, IT DOESN'T MEAN IT'S YOUR PROBLEM. IT'S THEIRS. QUIT PRETENDING THAT YOUR LIFE ISN'T PERFECT AND BITCHIN AND TELL THEM TO GO EARN THEIR OWN GODDAMN SLAMMIN LIVES. WE ARE HIGH PRIESTS OF SUCCESS AND, OH WAIT, THEY CAN'T PROCESS IT — LOSERS! NEVER FEEL BAD ABOUT **WINNING**.

I don't like my best friend's boyfriend.

TELL HER. IF SHE CAN'T HANDLE YOUR
VIOLENT TORPEDO OF TRUTH THEN
SHE'S NOT WORTHY OF YOU. AND HER
DOUCHEBAG BOYFRIEND DEFINITELY ISN'T.

All my friends are so much prettier and slimmer than me. I feel like the token 'ugly' one in our group and it's getting to be so demoralizing.

If cosmetic surgery ain't plausible then just DITCH THESE BITCHES and start hanging out with some real **TROLLS** to get a sense of **WINNING**. Onward and upward, sister, or — in your case — downward.

My friends are always saying that my girlfriend is way too hot for me and that I'm punching above my weight. It was funny at first, but they're always going on about it, and I know I'm not exactly smokin-hot, but it's starting to hurt now.

AWESOME. AWESOME. YOU'RE A TOP GUN
ROCKSTAR, BRO. WHAT'S TO FEEL BAD ABOUT?

SO THESE TROLLS ARE JEALOUS BECAUSE

YOU'RE **WINNING**. AND

WINNING HARD, BY THE

SOUND OF IT. SAY THIS TO

THEM NEXT TIME THEY OPEN

THEIR INSIGNIFICANT WHINY

MOUTHS ABOUT IT: 'WOW.

NOT ONLY DO I DESERVE

THIS, BUT. IT'S. ON. IT'S

ON LIKE DONKEY KONG.'

PEOPLE SAY IT'S LONELY AT
THE TOP, BUT I SURE
LIKE THE VIEW!

133

My roommate's boyfriend keeps touching me up when she leaves the room. I've told him to stop it, but he just laughs it off and carries on. I don't want to rock the boat by telling my friend in case she doesn't believe me.

TASER.

RANDOM

'IT'S OVER.
THERE'S A
NEW SHERIFF
IN TOWN,
AND HE
HAS AN
ARMY OF
ASSASSINS.'

I'm set to run my first marathon and the forecast is torrential rain. These conditions are less than perfect and so I'm tempted to defer my entry.

WWCSD?

DEFEATISM, THY NAME IS YOU. **DEFER?!!** IT'S LAME. IT'S RETARDED. IT'S TRANSPARENT. IT'S THE FREAKIN WORK OF **TROLLS.** 'DEFER' RHYMES WITH 'LOSER.' YOU'RE RUNNING THAT FREAKIN MARATHON IF I HAVE TO CHASE YOU ALL THE WAY WITH A **TASER.**

I'm fed up with not being able to get on the subway in the morning. It's always so packed.

You are an **F18**. You are a WARLOCK. There are parts of you that are **DENNIS HOPPER**. You have one speed, you have one gear: GO. Defeat is not an option: get on that train no matter what. **THRIVE ON CHAOS.**

I stole something from a clothes shop the other day. I don't know why I did it – I could afford to buy the item and I've never shoplifted before. Now I'm not sure whether to take it back to the shop and confess, or pretend it never happened.

THE KEY THING TO REMEMBER HERE IS THIS:
IT'S ONLY ILLEGAL IF YOU ADMIT
TO IT. YOU KNOW WHAT TO DO.

I'm going to be interviewed on live TV and am having huge trouble controlling my nerves. I've tried practicing my lines and doing yoga techniques but, as the date approaches, I'm getting more and more panicked.

WHY GIVE AN INTERVIEW WHEN YOU CAN LEAVE A **WARNING**? THAT'S © **CHARLIE SHEEN**, MY MAN. DO YOU WANNA STAY IN THE SHADOWS LIKE A LAME-ASS YOUR ENTIRE LIFE, OR BE IN THE EPICENTER OF BRILLIANCE? THIS IS A NO-BRAINER.

My parents want me to go to college, but I want to stay home with most of my friends and get a job. We're constantly fighting about it, but I don't know how to make them change their minds.

WWCSD?

Time to give your parents their own college lecture, kid, and it's this: **WINNERS** don't have go to college to **WIN**. I got expelled from high school, didn't go to college and — guess what? MY LIFE RULES. Remind them of the **CHARLIE SHEEN** story, and the situation will soon get resolved.

People walk all over me all the time. My friends, my family, my co-workers. I want to toughen up but don't want to turn into an asshole.

SINCE WHEN DOES BEING TOUGH MAKE SOMEONE AN ASSHOLE, BUDDY? HAVE YOU LEARNT NOTHING AT ALL FROM THESE PAGES? DO YOU NEED GLASSES? I'M TIRED OF LOSING ALL MY FREAKIN GOLD INTO THE ETHERSPHERE OF FREAKIN STUPIDITY. IT'S NOT ABOUT DEFEATING THE EARTHWORM WITH FIRE-BREATHING FISTS, BUT WITH WORDS. LIKE I DO. EVERY DAY. RESPECT YOURSELF AND YOU WILL DEMAND IT OF OTHERS.

*My life's a mess right now. I got sick. I lost my job.
I lost my house. And then I lost my girlfriend.
I don't know how to get my life back on track.*

A WISE MAN ONCE RAPPED 'I GOT 99 PROBLEMS
BUT A BITCH AIN'T ONE.' SOUNDS TO ME
LIKE YOU'VE GOT 100 PROBLEMS, BRO, AND D'YOU
KNOW WHAT'S NOT GONNA HELP YOU? **WHINING.**
LOSERS WHINE; **WINNERS WIN.**
IT'S ALL ABOUT ATTITUDE. I'VE SAID IT BEFORE
AND I'M JUST GONNA KEEP ON SAYING IT 'TIL
YOU PEOPLE TAKE THE HINT.
LIFE'S WHAT YOU MAKE OF IT. START **WINNING.**

GLOSSARY OF SHEENISMS

F18

A weasel-seeking man-missile, hell-bent on destruction.

GNARLY GNARLINGTON

You've got it sussed. And by 'it,' I mean life.

TIGER BLOOD

The stuff that runs through your veins when you're channelling pure SHEEN.

WINNING

If you're putting any of the advice in this book into practice, this is what you'll be doing. Guaranteed.

WARLOCK

Just the kind of awesome, kickass warrior that the Earth needs more of; think Dennis Hopper, Steven Seagal, Sly Stallone, and, of course, ME.

VATICAN ASSASSIN

Warlock in the employ of the most powerful religious organization on this planet. Also a trained killer.

GNARLY CADRE

A secret group of my super-loyal followers around the world. Cross ME, and you'll be hearing from them.

BITCHIN

Fantastic. Orgasmic. SHEEN all over.

ROCKSTAR

A person whose life you want to lead. Big time.

DUMBASS

A person whose life you <u>don't</u> want to lead. Steer clear of these losers. Full stop.

'DUDE, IT'S... IT'S SO IMPOSSIBLE. IT'S, LIKE, I DON'T HAVE **ANY ANSWERS**, MAN. I CAN'T TELL PEOPLE WHAT TO DO. I DON'T COME AT PEOPLE FROM A PLACE OF JUDGMENT OR OPINION. IF I'VE GOT SOME FACTS, THAT'S WHAT I STAND ON.'

What Would Charlie Sheen Do?
Researched, co-ordinated and
written by: S R Dawson

Designed by: Harriet Yeomans
Illustrations by: Jake Ayres
www.jakeayres.co.uk
www.facebook.com/jamegg.jlayres
Americanized by: Katie Bone
Proofread by: Leanne Bryan
Marketing: Shelley Bowdler
Publisher: Jonathan Knight

Published by: Punk Publishing,
3 The Yard, Pegasus Place,
London SE11 5SD

THANKS TO ...

Charlie Sheen, for being an inspirational
and exceedingly funny guy; Rob Dawson
and Amy Sheldrake for letting me
borrow a little of their winning advice;
Jake Ayres for his fantastic illustrations;
and Harriet Yeomans for being a
warlock when it comes to design.